FUNDAMENTALS OF POKER

by
Mason Malmuth and Lynne Loomis

A product of Two Plus Two Publishing

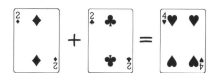

Second Edition

Printing and Binding
Creel Printing Company
Las Vegas, Nevada

Printed in the United States of America

ISBN: 1-880685-11-6

Dedicated to the Memory of
Walter I. Nolan
(1924-1987)

*Walter I. Nolan, whose initials form the acronym
WIN, was the pen name of the late John Luckman,
the founder of Gambler's Book Club. During his
illustrious career, Luckman not only wrote numerous
books and pamphlets on various gambling topics,
but also was directly responsible for bringing to
life many additional top-quality works by other gaming
authors. He is remembered for his integrity, his
adherence to high standards, and his devotion
to both the publishing and gaming industries.*

*It was with the hope of following the tradition
established by John Luckman that the* Fundamentals
of Poker *was written, and it is with honor and
reverence that this booklet is dedicated to the
memory of his literary pseudonym, Walter I. Nolan.*

Table of Contents

Introduction

Poker, in its many different forms, is one of the premier gambling games throughout the world. It offers excitement and action, demands great skill from an expert player, and contains a certain element of luck. But most of all, poker is fun to play.

This booklet discusses various aspects of the many different types of poker that are popular in casinos and public cardrooms. Emphasized most, however, are seven-card stud and Texas hold'em, as these two forms of poker are the most widely played. Other games covered in the *Fundamentals of Poker* are Omaha hold'em, Omaha eight-or-better, seven-card stud eight-or-better, razz, and lowball draw.

In today's cardrooms, the limits range from very small to extremely large, where thousands of dollars can cross the table in the course of one hand. But to help you get started at playing poker, we have concentrated on the low-limit games.

Poker tournaments also have become popular in recent years. The most prestigious is the World Series of Poker, which is held at Binion's Horseshoe in Las Vegas, Nevada, where a new world champion is crowned each May. Major poker tournaments also are hosted by the large card casinos of Southern California, and countless small events are regularly scheduled in legal cardrooms throughout the United States and in many foreign countries.

The wide array of live-action games and competitive events available continues to promote the increasing popularity of poker. And since the game is not only fun but also potentially profitable, it is well worth learning to play.

The authors wish to thank the following individuals for their advice and assistance: Jim Albrecht, Binion's Horseshoe; Mike Byrne, Fort McDowell Gaming Center; Donna Harris, The Mirage; and John Sutton, formerly of The Bicycle Club. Also, special thanks to Terry Cannon, Dan Harrington, David Sklansky, Steve Stamler, and Ray Zee.

A Brief History

The exact origin of poker is unknown. However, its roots appear to lie in a 16th-century Persian card game called As Nas and in the European card game of Primero, which was quite popular in Elizabethan England. As Nas was played with 20 cards, and bluffing was an important element of the game. Primero, or Primera as it was called in Spain, involved betting and valued hands, including pairs, three of a kind, and three of the same suit, referred to as a "flux." The derivative "flush" is the modern-day term for a suited poker hand.

By the 18th century, the betting and bluffing aspects of poker were present in several five-card games, including the English game of Brag, the German game of Pochen (the word "pochen" means "to bluff"), and the French game called Poque.

When French colonists arrived to settle the Louisiana territory in the 1700s, they brought poque with them, and the name of the game was eventually modified to the American term "poker." The game took hold around the city of New Orleans, and in the early 1800s, it began to spread north, as steamboats plied the Mississippi River, transporting goods and passengers to inland ports.

By the mid-1800s, poker had been adapted to a 52-card deck and was described in books about card games. Poker continued to spread as the West was settled, and its popularity mushroomed during the Civil War, when Union soldiers were exposed to the game as they moved southward.

Poker was firmly entrenched in America by the turn of the century and was played virtually everywhere throughout the United States, as well as in many foreign countries. The games played were draw poker, a form of closed poker, where all of the cards are dealt face down, and stud poker, where the hands are open — that is, some of the cards are dealt face up.

In the early 1900s, a new form of open poker began to appear. Known as Texas hold'em, it became widely played throughout the South, especially in the state of Texas. Although stud arrived in Las Vegas when gambling was legalized in the 1930s, hold'em was not introduced in Nevada to any noticeable extent until the early 1970s.

Two catalysts were responsible for the rapid growth in popularity of this game. The first was the prestigious World Series of Poker, which in 1970 adopted Texas hold'em as the game to determine the world champion. The second catalyst was a book titled *Hold'em Poker*, written by noted gambling authority and poker expert David Sklansky. Published in 1976, this text was the first to quantify Texas hold'em and thus make the game accessible to the average poker player.

As for draw poker, it faded away, except in California, where it was the only form of poker legal until 1987. Now that stud and hold'em are also legal in the Golden State, high draw has become virtually extinct, and lowball draw seems to be slowly disappearing.

Currently, the two dominant forms of poker in the United States are seven-card stud and Texas hold'em, although many additional types of poker are played in legal cardrooms across the nation, as well as in other countries. In its present format, poker is thought of as uniquely American, yet its appeal is international, and today, poker ranks among the most popular card games in the world.

General Guidelines

THE BASICS OF POKER

The basic rules of poker are simple. The objective of the game is to win the pot — that is, the money or chips placed in the center of the table. This is accomplished in one of two ways. Either you can show your opponents the best hand — which may be a high hand or a low hand, depending on the particular variation of poker that you are playing — or you can bluff and convince them you have the best hand. In some forms of poker, the best high hand and the best low hand each win half the pot. This variation is known as a split-pot game.

Each poker hand is begun by seeding the pot with a token amount of money in the form of an ante or one or more blind bets. If an ante is used, everyone must put a small percentage of the initial bet into the pot. If blinds are used, one or more players will be designated to post a bet or a partial bet before receiving any cards. Blinds usually are rotated around the table, so everyone pays his fair share.

During the play of a hand, opportunities to bet and raise occur after each round of cards is dealt. If at any time you choose not to continue in the hand, you may discard it, thus forfeiting your interest in the pot. This means, of course, that you do not have to put any additional money into the pot.

If you are the bettor or raiser and no one calls your last bet, you win the pot. If one or more players do call, then the person with the best hand wins the pot.

Poker is as simple as that. Yet this basic set of rules, plus a few additional ones specific to each form of poker, produces a most wonderful game. A game that many people will play for a lifetime — some very seriously, but countless others for enjoyment alone.

THE RANKING OF HANDS

Seven-card stud and Texas hold'em are variations of high poker, where the highest ranking hand wins. These two games and most other forms of poker are played with a standard 52-card deck. No joker is included. A deck consists of four different suits (all suits being equal) — spades, hearts, diamonds, and clubs — and each suit contains 13 cards. The ace is the highest ranking card, followed by the king, queen, jack, ten, nine, eight, seven, six, five, four, trey, and deuce. An ace also may be used as the lowest ranking card in a five-high straight — for example, A♦2♠3♣4♥5♠ — or in a five-high straight flush, such as A♥2♥3♥4♥5♥.

Although most forms of poker addressed in this booklet are played with seven cards, the goal is to make the best five-card poker hand at the showdown. The ranking order for hands in high poker, based on their probability of occurrence — from least likely to most likely — is as follows:

Straight flush — five cards of the same suit in sequence. An ace-high straight flush is referred to as a "royal flush" and is the best possible hand in high poker.

Four of a kind — four cards of the same rank, plus an unrelated fifth card that has no bearing on the hand's value. The higher the rank of the four of a kind, the better the hand is.

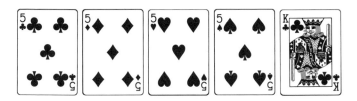

Full house — three cards of one rank and two cards of another other rank. The rank of a full house is determined by the three of a kind, not by the pair.

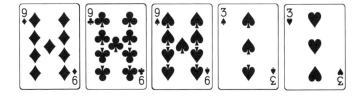

Flush — any five cards of the same suit. The cards are not in sequence, and the suit has no bearing on the rank of the flush. If more than one player holds a flush, the highest flush is determined by the rank of the individual cards, starting with the highest card.

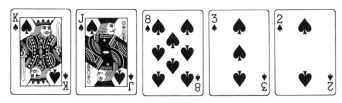

Straight — five cards in sequence, not all of the same suit.

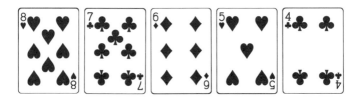

Three of a kind — three cards of the same rank, plus two unrelated cards.

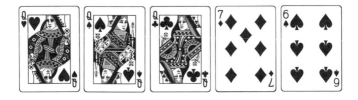

Two pair — two cards of one rank, two cards of another rank, and one unrelated card. If two players each have two pair and their high pair is of the same rank, the winning hand is determined by the rank of the lower pair. If both lower pair are also of the same rank, then the winning hand is determined by the rank of the unrelated card.

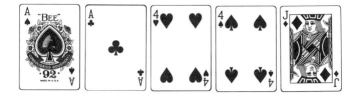

One pair — two cards of one rank, plus three unrelated cards. If two players hold the same rank of one pair, the rank of their side cards determines the best hand.

No pair — five unrelated cards.

As a reminder, in the event that two or more hands tie in a particular category, the winning hand is determined by the rank of the unrelated cards. Also, all suits are of equal value for determining hand rankings at the showdown.

The hand rankings listed are for high poker only. But in some forms of poker, the best low hand wins the pot, and in other forms — known as split-pot games — the best low hand, with certain qualifications, wins half the pot. Several of these games are discussed in this booklet. In all of them, the best low hand is ace-deuce-trey-four-five, which is known as a wheel or a bicycle, and straights and flushes are disregarded for low.

In addition, the only form of closed poker we discuss — lowball draw — is played with a standard 52-card deck, plus a joker, which counts as the lowest card not already in a player's hand.

GENERAL ADVICE

As we've emphasized, casino poker can be a great deal of fun. That's why so many people play it. But poker is complex, and many players are very competitive. This means that to do well in the game, you must be able to play at your best. What follows are a few general tips that should be helpful to you in this area.

Tip No. 1: Maintain a positive attitude. A good attitude translates into patience and discipline. Sometimes you won't get your fair share of good playable hands, and this can be frustrating. But if your attitude becomes negative, you may find yourself playing hands you should have thrown away, plus making other costly errors.

Tip No. 2: Recognize the short-term luck factor in poker. To play poker well requires a lot of skill, yet the game contains a large element of luck in the short run. Good players will beat bad players, but not necessarily the next time you play. And seeing a poor player win many hands in a short period of time can be discouraging, especially if you were involved in some of those pots. But this short-term luck is part of poker and, in fact, is one of the factors that keeps the games thriving. Sometimes you will be the player who gets lucky. When this happens, you are said to be on a "rush," which is a terrific feeling.

Tip No. 3: Be well-rested when you play. You must make a lot of decisions when playing poker, and determining the best course of action is often difficult. Although experience helps in this area, being able to think clearly and quickly are extremely important. If you are tired, you may make a few mistakes that you ordinarily would not make, and these errors easily can be the difference between winning and losing.

Tip No. 4: Drink in moderation. There's nothing wrong with drinking socially while playing poker. But many players drink too much and then begin to make bad decisions. An inebriated player typically plays too many hands, goes too far with his hands, calls too many bets and raises, overplays his reasonably good holdings, and otherwise makes decisions associated with bad play.

Tip No. 5: Enjoy the game. Poker is fun to play, but as noted, it can be quite frustrating at times, partly because of the short-term luck factor. If you become discouraged and lose your patience and discipline, you may discover that you are making too many mistakes to be successful. So sit back, relax, and enjoy playing the game.

Tip No. 6: Be cautious of playing in a game if you are uncomfortable with the stakes. Should you play with your rent money? Of course not. First, you might lose it, and that can be a big problem. Second, if you play at a limit you are not comfortable with, the pressure may cause you to make costly mistakes, or at the very least, you won't play your best game.

Tip No. 7: Always play your best. Sometimes when you see poor players making critical mistakes and still winning, you may be tempted to imitate their play. Don't do it. Remember, despite the short-term luck factor, poker is a game of skill, and good players will beat bad players in the long run.

Tip No. 8: Protect your hand. When you first begin to play poker, it's important to remember to conceal your cards so that no one else can see them. After playing for a short while, this should become second nature. Needless to say, if someone knows what you hold, it will be almost impossible to win, no matter how well you play.

It is also important to hold on to your cards or to put a chip on top of them, so the dealer won't mistakenly think you have discarded your hand. In addition, you should turn your cards face up at the showdown, so the dealer can read your hand to see if you have won the pot. Otherwise, you might discover that instead of winning the pot, your hand has been mucked — that is, discarded — by the dealer.

POKER ETIQUETTE

Although poker is a pleasurable pastime, it is enjoyable only when the game runs smoothly and quickly. Most of the responsibility for ensuring this rests with the house dealer, but players can do their part to keep the game moving in an orderly fashion. So you will know what is expected of you at the poker table, we are providing the following "rules" of poker etiquette.

Rule No. 1: Act in turn. In poker, the action proceeds clockwise around the table, one player at a time. Acting out of turn not only shows a basic disregard of propriety, but also may give a player an unfair advantage over his remaining opponents. As an example, discarding your hand before the action gets to you may tell a player who should have acted ahead of you that it is now easier for him to get away with a bluff. This obviously is not fair to those players who already have chosen not to bet.

Rule No. 2: Don't throw your chips into the pot. Throwing your chips directly into the pot, also known as "splashing the pot," makes it difficult for the dealer and other players to determine whether you have bet the correct amount. In fact, when a player splashes the pot, it sometimes may be necessary for the dealer to interrupt play and count down the pot to make sure it is correct. The proper way to make your bet is to place it directly in front of you on the table. The dealer will inspect your bet for accuracy and then will add it to the other chips in the center of the table.

Rule No. 3: Avoid making a "string bet" or "string raise." When you bet or raise, you should place the proper amount of chips in the pot at one time. A string bet/raise is an illegal play and occurs when a player places less than the full raise in the pot and, without verbally announcing a raise, returns to his stack to get more chips. This play is prohibited, as an unscrupulous player can use it to his advantage. As a precaution, always say, "Raise," when you intend to raise.

Rule No. 4: Make decisions in a timely manner. Most starting hands in poker are thrown away, which means that a great deal of your time is spent watching, not playing. Thus you want your opponents to play as fast as possible, and you should do the same. This doesn't mean that when you're faced with a tough decision, you can't take some time to figure it out. In fact, if you need a moment, say, "Time, please." But whenever possible, act on your hand quickly.

Rule No. 5: Keep your cards on the table. Most cardrooms prohibit you from taking your cards off the table. However, it's important to keep your cards in front of you for two additional reasons. First, when you pick up your hand, it may be seen by a player sitting next to you, which gives him an unfair advantage. Second, the dealer usually looks down and in front of you. If he doesn't see your hand, he may deal your next card to someone else on a later round, causing confusion.

Rule No. 6: Turn all of your cards face up at the showdown. This is necessary so the dealer can read your hand to determine whether you've won the pot. In addition, the other players will see that you have a legitimate hand made up of seven different cards. If you turn up only the five cards that you think make the best hand, not only will the other players object, but also you may have missed seeing the winning hand. Needless to say, if no one calls your final bet or raise, it's not necessary to show your cards.

Rule No. 7: Don't discuss your hand during play. Providing information about your hand to other players, even if you have thrown your cards away, may give someone an unfair advantage. For example, if you abandon your hand and then remark, "I just threw away an ace and a king," a player holding one of these cards now may choose not to enter the pot with a hand he otherwise would have played.

Rule No. 8: The games are played "table stakes." This means that only the money and chips you have in front of you on the table are in play. If you run out of money during the play of a hand, you are said to be "all in" and can contest only the part of the pot that your bets cover. You are not allowed to reach into your pocket and produce more money during that hand. (Notice that you will not lose the pot because someone has bet more money than you currently have on the table.) In addition, you are not permitted to remove money from the table until you are ready to leave the game.

Rule No. 9: Tipping is appreciated. Though not obligatory, it's customary to give the dealer a tip when you win an average-sized pot. Tipping is an accepted way of thanking the dealer for performing his job in a professional and courteous manner.

ELEMENTAL POKER CONCEPTS

Although each individual form of poker has specific strategies that apply primarily to that game, certain basic themes and ideas are universal to all of poker. Consequently, a good understanding of the concepts that follow will be helpful, no matter what form of poker you choose to play.

Concept No. 1: Play in loose games whenever possible. Regardless of how well you play poker, to be a consistent winner, you must play in good games. And good games are usually those games with many players in most pots. The reason a loose game is considered "good" is that some players frequently will enter the pot with hands they should have thrown away. Incidentally, the majority of low-limit games are fairly loose.

Concept No. 2: Be selective of the hands you play. With a full table of players, there is an excellent chance that someone will make a good hand. As a result, if you play most of the hands you are dealt, you can't expect to be a winner in the long run.

Concept No. 3: Play aggressively. Poker is not a game for weak, passive players. If you neglect to bet, an opponent who might have thrown his cards away may get lucky and receive a card that beats you. Moreover, if you bet only when you have a very strong hand, your opponents will know you have a good hand and won't call you unless they also have a strong holding.

Concept No. 4: Bluff some, but not too much. This is actually a continuation of the concept just mentioned. If you never bluff — that is, never bet a hand that has virtually no chance of winning in a showdown — many of your opponents will learn that you bet only your better hands. Again, they will call you only when they also happen to be holding a strong hand.

Similarly, you shouldn't bluff too much. There are two reasons for this. First, bluffing typical opponents just a small percentage of the time gains the desired effect. Second, some of your opponents will call too much, especially at the lower limits. Bluffing this type of player can be suicide for your bankroll.

Concept No. 5: Position is important. Acting last is an advantage in virtually all forms of poker, as you will have gained information about your opponents' hands, but they will not have gained that same information about your hand. Good position allows you to play more hands, bet more hands, escape traps — for example, you may throw away a marginal hand when someone else bets or raises — and even bluff more.

Concept No. 6: Adjust your play, depending on your opponents. Poker is a people game. Who you are against and how they play can make a critical difference. For instance, against someone who bluffs a lot, you should be willing to call with weak hands; against someone who generally never bluffs, you should call only with very strong hands. In addition, an opponent's mood may change, depending on how he is doing in the game. When this occurs, it's as though you are against an entirely different person, and you should adjust your play accordingly.

Concept No. 7: The larger the pot, the more you should call. Just because it is unlikely that you have the best hand doesn't always mean that you should discard it. As an example, suppose that after all the cards are out, your opponent bets $4, which increases the pot to a total of $36. Since it will cost you only $4 to call, your hand needs to be the best just one out of 10 times for your call to be correct. In other words, you are getting 36-to-4 or 9-to-1 pot odds. Even if you have just a small chance of winning, you frequently should make this call.

Concept No. 8: Observe the action. When not involved in a hand, spend your time wisely. Observe those opponents involved in the hand in order to ascertain their playing habits.

Seven-Card Stud

INTRODUCTION

Seven-card stud is an intricate game that requires much patience and concentration. Though it can be dispiriting at times, since the best starting hand frequently gets beat, stud still offers a great deal of action that makes the game exciting and fun to play.

There are two critical decisions that you must make when playing seven-card stud. The first occurs on the first betting round, which is known as third street, and is simply whether to enter the pot. If you make this decision well, you should be able to beat most low-limit stud games — providing, that is, that the rest of your game is adequate.

The second crucial decision you must make is whether to continue playing on the third betting round, which is referred to as fifth street. This is the last opportunity you will have to profitably throw away your hand. If you continue to play a hand on fifth street that you should have discarded, you easily can be trapped for three double-sized bets.

Of course, every decision you make in seven-card stud is important, and any mistake can prove to be costly. However, your ability to ascertain the best course of action on third and fifth streets is the primary factor that will determine whether you are a winner or a loser in this game.

As you will see, to become an expert at seven-card stud requires numerous poker skills, many of which are beyond the scope of this booklet. But the information that follows should be helpful in ensuring your success in the low-limit games.

HOW TO PLAY

In seven-card stud, each player generally posts an ante prior to the cards being dealt (although some low-limit games require no ante). To begin the hand, all players are dealt two downcards and one upcard. The player with the lowest upcard is required to start the action on the first betting round with a small bet, which is called the bring-in. If more than one player has the same rank of low card, then suit in alphabetical order — clubs, diamonds, hearts, spades — determines who must start the action.

The first player to the left of the bring-in has three options: He may throw away his hand, call the bring-in, or raise to a full bet. If he folds or calls the bring-in, the person to his left has the same options; however, if the first player raises to a full bet, the next person now has the options of folding, calling the full bet, or raising again. The action proceeds clockwise in this manner until all players have exercised their options and all bets have been called.

All players remaining in the hand then receive three more upcards and a final card face down, with a betting round after each card is dealt. In these subsequent four betting rounds, the player with the high hand on board acts first. If two hands are of equal high value, the player to the left of the dealer initiates the betting action. At the showdown, the player who makes the best five-card poker hand from the seven cards he possesses wins the pot.

Structured-limit or fixed-limit seven-card stud games have a double limit, with the lower limit used in the early betting rounds and the higher limit (which is usually double the lower limit) used in the later rounds. Thus the lower bet is allowed on the first and second betting rounds — referred to as third street and fourth street — which correspond to the first three cards and the fourth card, and a double-sized bet is required on the third, fourth, and fifth betting rounds. These later rounds correspond to the fifth, sixth, and seventh cards, and are called, respectively, fifth street, sixth street, and seventh street, or the river. There is one exception: If a player has an open pair on fourth street, either a single or a double-sized bet may be made.

Here's an example. Suppose you are playing $3-$6 seven-card stud. Everyone will ante 50 cents, the player with the low card will bring it in for $1, and the first player to his left will have the options of folding, calling the $1 bring-in, or raising to $3. Once the bet has been raised to $3, all subsequent bets and raises on both third and fourth streets will be in $3 increments, unless a player makes an open pair on fourth street. In this case, any active player has the options of betting or raising either $3 or $6. All bets and raises on the last three betting rounds will be in $6 increments. Typically, cardrooms allow three or four raises. But heads up (two players), the number of raises is unlimited.

Many low-stakes seven-card stud games also are played with spread limits, where each player has the option to bet or raise an amount that is not fixed. As an example, in a typical $1-$4 spread-limit stud game, there is no ante, the low card brings it in for $1, and all bets and raises can be any amount from $1 to $4 at the bettor's discretion.

Finally, in some low-limit stud games, a jackpot is awarded when a very strong hand gets beat by an even better hand. To seed the jackpot pool, the house usually sets aside a small amount of money from each pot, although sometimes an additional ante is required to support the jackpot. When a good hand, such as aces full of queens, gets beat, the player holding the losing hand wins either the entire jackpot or a large percentage of it. In most cardrooms, the player holding the winning hand also receives a portion of the jackpot, and sometimes all players dealt in the hand are awarded a token amount of the prize money.

Jackpot poker is currently very popular in California card clubs and has begun to catch on in some of the cardrooms in Nevada and other places where poker is legal.

Depending on the game, typical jackpots range from $2,000 to $10,000, but some have exceeded $50,000.

STRATEGY TIPS

As we have stated, seven-card stud is an intricate game, and determining the best possible play in a given situation involves numerous factors. So before we get into specifics on what hands to play and how you should play them, following are a few tips that will help you make the correct decisions.

Tip No. 1: Play live hands. Seven-card stud, as its name implies, is a seven-card game. Consequently, you should play hands that have a good chance to improve. For example, if you start with three cards of the same suit — called a three flush — and several other cards of this suit are out on board, your hand is said to be dead and therefore should be thrown away. By the same token, if only one or two of your suited cards are showing, you have a hand of value that should be played in most situations.

Tip No. 2: Big pairs play better against only one or two opponents, while drawing hands prefer lots of company. A hand like

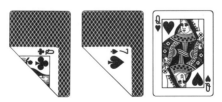

and a hand like

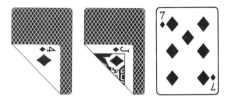

are both good hands, but they play much differently. Big pairs usually do best when played in short-handed pots, because against only a few opponents, a big pair has a reasonable chance of winning without improvement.

The opposite is true of the drawing hands, such as a three flush or a three straight. Although these are good starting hands, they have no immediate value. Moreover, you will not complete your flush or straight very often. You therefore prefer to have many opponents, so that when you do make your hand, someone will still be around to pay it off.

Tip No. 3: Small and medium pairs are much worse than big pairs. A hand like

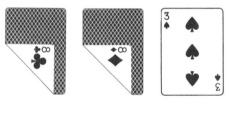

and even a hand like

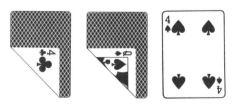

are occasionally good hands. But in general, there is a big difference in strength between these hands and the big pairs. For example, when you play a small or medium pair, one of your opponents easily can catch a card higher than your pair, which might give him a bigger pair that will beat you.

Tip No. 4: Having one or more high cards adds value to your hand. We have just touched on this. Holding a high card allows you to catch another card of the same rank, which might be enough to win the pot. Having more than one high card is even better.

Tip No. 5: Be aware — and beware — of scare cards. A scare card is a card that either improves your hand or allows you to catch another card that will improve your hand. For example, catching a suited jack on fourth street to go along with a king adds enormous value to your hand. Your opponent now has to worry about a possible straight or flush, as well as a possible big pair. Likewise, you need to be concerned when your opponent catches a scare card.

Tip No. 6: It is often correct to chase. Even though you should be selective of the hands you play, once you enter a pot, it is often correct to go all the way. This is sometimes true even when you are sure you don't have the best hand. Of course, if your hand becomes hopeless, you should discard it. But in many situations, you will have enough ways to win that chasing is worthwhile.

STARTING HANDS

There are four main categories of starting hands in seven-card stud: three of a kind, also referred to as rolled-up trips; big pairs; small and medium pairs; and the drawing hands. There are also some other hands that you occasionally should play, but a discussion of them is beyond the scope of this booklet. However, the starting hand quiz that follows this section provides a few tips on how to play some of these additional hands.

Category No. 1: Three of a kind. This is the best starting hand in seven-card stud, but you won't get it very often — in fact, on the average of only once in every 425 times you are dealt in.

Because rolled-up trips are so strong, it usually doesn't matter how you play them. Still, you don't want to be dealt three queens and win only the antes. So if you are in an early position and think a raise will drive out the other players, you should just call. On the other hand, if several players are already in the pot before the action gets to you, your raise is unlikely to make them fold. But remember, although three of a kind is a powerful hand, it is not invincible and occasionally does get beat.

Category No. 2: Big pairs. The big pairs are almost always playable and should be played aggressively. The exception is if you are likely to be up against someone who holds a larger pair. In this case, you should consider throwing your hand away, unless your kicker — the side card to your pair — is higher than your opponent's probable pair.

When you play a big pair, you generally go all the way to the river. However, if your opponent pairs his third-street card (known as the door card) or makes something else threatening — such as a four flush on board — you should fold.

Category No. 3: Small and medium pairs. Determining whether to play a small or medium pair can be fairly complicated. The two most important considerations are the availability of the cards you need — that is, whether your hand is live — and the size of your kicker. As already noted, a high card can add value to your hand. Nevertheless, playing a pair of fours when you can see a four across the table is usually a mistake — even if your kicker is an ace.

Category No. 4: The drawing hands. Hands such as three flushes and three straights are often playable. Again, the cards you need must be available, and having a high card is helpful in determining whether to play heads up. Unlike the pairs, drawing hands have no present value; you play them because they have the potential to become very strong.

STARTING HAND QUIZ

1. You have been dealt two aces, one in the hole and one up. What should you do?

Raise or reraise when the action gets to you. A pair of aces plays best in a short-handed pot, so raise it up.

2. You have been dealt a three flush, but four of the flush cards you need are out and someone has already raised. What should you do?

Throw your hand away, as it's just too difficult to make your flush.

3. What if the pot is not raised?

For the same reason, you still should throw your three flush away.

4. You have only three high cards, but the first five players have mucked their hands. What should you do?

Go ahead and raise.

5. What if several players have already entered the pot?

Throw your hand away. High cards play best against a small number of opponents.

6. Someone in an early position raises with a king up, and you have a pair of nines. Do you play?

Not usually, as your opponent's raise from early position indicates that he likely holds a pair of kings. Consequently, to play under these circumstances, you need more than just a pair of nines.

7. You have a small three straight with a gap. You are in a late position, and several players have just called the bring-in. Do you play?

Usually. If you can get in cheaply and are fairly certain you won't be raised, you can play some weaker hands. However, be careful. If you get caught up in the action, you will begin to play too many hands.

8. You have rolled-up sixes, and three players have already entered the pot. What should you do?

Raise it up. You have a great hand, so get more money into the pot.

9. Several players are already in, and you have a three flush. Should you raise?

No, as you still have a long way to go. Raise only if you have three cards to a straight flush.

10. Suppose you have a small buried pair and the pot is raised. Do you play?

Only if there are several players in the pot and your cards are live.

11. When you have a close decision concerning whether to play a hand, what should you consider?

How well those opponents already in the pot play. The better they play, the less inclined you should be to play.

12. How do you adjust the hands you should play if a jackpot is offered?

If the jackpot is small, you should not play any differently than you normally would. But when the jackpot has become large, it makes sense to play hands that contain a small pair or an ace if aces full or better is the required losing hand. If four of a kind is the required losing hand, you should play your small pairs. But don't get carried away. A hand like

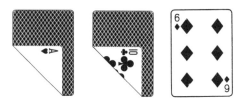

is still terrible and should be discarded.

PLAY ON THE LATER STREETS

Even though the most important decision you will make in seven-card stud is on third street, you don't want to neglect the later streets. Winning depends on correctly assessing an infinite number of situations, and errors in judgment can spell disaster. The tips that follow will help you to recognize and take advantage of profitable opportunities, as well as to dodge the perils, often encountered on fourth street and beyond.

Tip No. 1: It is very dangerous when an opponent pairs his door card. When this happens, you should exercise caution, as there is a good chance that your opponent now has three of a kind. And even if he doesn't have trips, he's still likely to hold a quality hand. So unless your hand is also of high value or the pot is very large, you should throw your cards away.

Tip No. 2: If you make what appears to be the best hand on a later street, you should bet out. In seven-card stud, it is generally a mistake to check a hand that you think is the best. For example, suppose you make a flush on sixth street. Since some of your suited cards are exposed, your opponent will suspect a flush, and if you check, he will check behind you. As a result, you not only might lose a double-sized bet, but the free card you give may cost you the pot as well.

Tip No. 3: It is sometimes correct to check and call. Suppose your opponent catches a third suited card and you think he may now have a flush. Although you should be aggressive in many situations, this is not one of them. The correct play here is to check and call. If your opponent does have a flush, you save money, since you don't have to call a raise; if he doesn't have a flush, he often will bet to represent one, so the money goes into the pot anyway.

Tip No. 4: You usually should call on fifth street when you have a small pair and a high overcard to an opponent's probable pair. In seven-card stud, it is often correct to chase, particularly when your hand has a strong potential of beating the hand you are up against. This means that you should call a fifth-street bet from a probable high pair when you have a smaller pair and an overcard kicker — especially if your kicker is an ace — as long as your hand is live and you have no reason to believe your opponent has two pair.

Tip No. 5: If you go to sixth street, almost always go to the river. In general, if you have called the fifth-street bet, it is correct to also call the bet on sixth street and look at the last card. The reason for this is that the pot typically has grown large enough and you usually have enough ways to win — even with a weak holding — that it is profitable to call. As an example, two small pair will win against a high pair that fails to improve on the river. However, if your opponent makes something extremely threatening on sixth street and your hand is weak, it obviously is correct to fold.

Tip No. 6: If you can beat a bluff, you usually should call on seventh street. Unless your hand is completely hopeless, folding on the river can be a costly mistake. You have to catch a bluff only once in a while for your calls to be correct. This is because the typical seven-card stud pot is large relative to the last bet.

SPREAD LIMIT
STRATEGY CHANGES

Most of the strategy already discussed for structured-limit games also applies to spread-limit games. However, there are a couple of basic differences.

First, you should be willing to play a lot of weak hands for just the bring-in — typically either 50 cents or $1 in a $1-$4 seven-card stud game. But remember to consider your position. If you are early to act and a lot of high cards are behind you, it is still best to throw away all weak hands, even if the cost to enter the pot is only 50 cents. In most cases, you also should discard speculative hands if someone raises after you have called the bring-in.

The second major difference in strategy concerns raising. When you have a good hand, you definitely want some opponents. So you generally should not raise the maximum on third street if no one has yet voluntarily entered the pot. Wait for the later rounds to bet the maximum.

For example, suppose you have a big pair and no one is in the pot yet, except for the bring-in. In this situation, it is usually best to raise only $2 instead of the $4 maximum to ensure that you get some competition. You don't want to win just 50 cents with a pair of aces.

SELECTED ODDS

Knowing the precise odds is not necessary to be a successful poker player. All you need is a good understanding of your chances in a given set of circumstances. This being said, what follows are some of the more useful odds for seven-card stud, which are provided mainly for their interest alone.

The First Three Cards

Starting Hand	Odds
Three of a Kind	424-to-1
A Pair of Aces	76-to-1
Any Pair	5-to-1
Three Suited Cards	18-to-1

Other Odds of Interest

- If you start with three suited cards, the odds against making a flush are 4.5-to-1.

- If you have four suited cards on fourth street, the odds against making a flush are 1.5-to-1, but with only three suited cards on fourth street, the odds increase to 8.5-to-1.

- If you start with a pair, the odds against making two pair are 1.4-to-1, and the odds against making three of a kind or better are 4.1-to-1.

- If you start with three of a kind, the odds against making a full house or better are 1.5-to-1.

Texas Hold'em

INTRODUCTION

Texas hold'em is a fast and exciting form of poker. The game is also surprisingly complex and requires a great deal of skill to play at the expert level. It's no wonder, then, that hold'em has rapidly become one of the most popular forms of poker in cardrooms around the country.

To the uneducated eye, Texas hold'em appears to be very similar to seven-card stud, but in fact, there are several critical differences between the two games. To begin with, the starting hand decision in hold'em, though very important, is not the dominating factor that it is in stud. If you do not also play reasonably well on the later streets, the best you can hope for in hold'em is to break even in the long run.

Hold'em is also more of a positional game than seven-card stud, because the order of betting does not change from round to round. In addition, a hold'em starting hand consists of just two cards instead of three cards. This means that you have less of an idea in the beginning of how strong your hand ultimately will be after all seven cards have been dealt.

But perhaps the most important difference between the two games is that Texas hold'em uses community cards, which are dealt face up in the center of the table and are part of each active player's hand. This makes it much more difficult to draw out on an opponent. As an example, if you start with two kings, your opponent starts with two aces, and a pair appears on board, you both have two pair. When you make two pair in seven-card stud, you frequently will beat a lone higher pair. This does not occur as often in Texas hold'em.

HOW TO PLAY

In Texas hold'em, a small flat disk, called a "button," is used to indicate the dealer position. Prior to the cards being dealt, the first player to the left of the dealer position posts a small blind, and the second player to the dealer's left puts up a big blind, which usually is equal to the first-round bet. Blinds are "live" bets, which signifies two things. First, a blind is a "real" bet, and to enter the pot, a player in a blind position needs only to make up the difference, if any, between his blind and the current bet. Second, players in the blinds have the option of raising when the action gets back to them, even if there has been no prior raise. When each hand is completed, the dealer button is moved one position to the left, and the procedure of posting blinds is repeated, so everyone pays his fair share.

To start the hand, each player, beginning with the small blind, receives two cards dealt face down one at a time. Action is initiated on the first betting round by the player to the immediate left of the big blind, who has the options of discarding his hand, calling the big blind, or raising an equivalent amount. The action moves clockwise in this manner until all players have exercised their options and all bets have been called. On all subsequent betting rounds, the first active player to the left of the dealer button starts the action.

After the first round of betting is completed, three cards — referred to as "the flop" — are turned face up simultaneously in the center of the table, and another round of betting occurs. The next two board cards — specified as either fourth street and fifth street or the turn card and the river card — are then dealt face up one at a time in the center of the table, with a betting round after each card. As noted previously, these board cards are community cards and are shared by all active players in the hand.

At the showdown, the player who makes the best five-card poker hand, using any combination of the five cards on board and the two cards in his hand, wins the pot. In Texas hold'em, more than one player often will have the best hand. When this happens, the pot is split.

Fixed-limit hold'em games have a two-tiered betting structure, with the lower limit used in the first two betting rounds and the higher limit (which is usually double the lower limit) used in the final two rounds of betting. As an example, suppose you are playing in a $3-$6 hold'em game. The first player to the left of the dealer position will put in a $1 small blind, and the second player to the dealer's left will post a $3 big blind. On the first round of betting, the player to the immediate left of the big blind will have the options of discarding his hand, calling the $3 big blind, or raising $3, for a total bet of $6. Subsequent bets and raises both before the flop and on the flop will be in $3 increments. All bets and raises on fourth and fifth streets must be in $6 increments.

Many low-stakes Texas hold'em games are also played with spread limits, which means that any player has the option of betting or raising an amount that is not fixed. For instance, in a typical $1-$4-$8 spread-limit hold'em game, there will be either two $1 blinds or one $2 blind. The first player to the left of the blind(s) can fold, call the blind, or raise any amount from $1 to $4. Subsequent bets and raises on the first three betting rounds can be from $1 to $4 at the player's discretion. Bets and raises on the final round of betting can be any amount from $1 to $8.

Many cardrooms throughout the country award jackpots in Texas hold'em games, as well as in seven-card stud games. The procedure used for seeding the jackpot pool and the tips for playing in a hold'em game that offers a jackpot are the same as those given previously in the section on seven-card stud.

STRATEGY TIPS

Texas hold'em is deceptive. It appears easy to play, yet beneath that simple facade lies a game of extraordinary complexity. Many variables must be considered when making decisions, and figuring out the correct play is often difficult. So before we discuss specific hands and how they generally should be played, here are some tips that will help you determine the best course of action.

Tip No. 1: Know what the best possible hand is and how likely it is to be out. With certain upcards, the potential for many different strong hands increases. With other upcards, however, the number of combinations is dramatically reduced. For example, if the board is

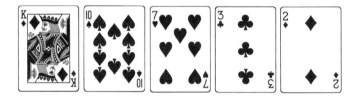

no one can have a straight, a flush, or a full house. The best possible hand is three kings.

Whether someone is holding the best possible hand — which in the poker vernacular is referred to as "the nuts" — frequently can be determined by the number of players in the pot and the previous action. The more players there are and the more betting and raising that have taken place, the more likely it is that one of your opponents has the nuts.

Tip No. 2: Recognize when you hold the best possible hand. Although this tip is actually a continuation of the one just given, its importance is such that it rates a separate listing. If you have the nuts and fail to recognize it, you will miss betting and raising opportunities, which in turn will cost you money. And thinking you have the best possible hand when you don't can be even more expensive. However, by paying close attention to the board, you will avoid making these costly errors. As an example, if the board is

and you hold ace-king, you can't be beat. You therefore should get as much money as possible into the pot. But if the board shows the 3 ♦ instead of the 3 ♠, you can lose to a flush and should proceed with caution.

Tip No. 3: Position is significant. Texas hold'em is known as a fixed-position game as opposed to a random-position game. In other words, the order in which the players act each round is predetermined, rather than determined by the strength of the exposed cards as it is in stud. We have already noted the advantage of acting last in poker. This means that you should be more selective of the hands you play in early position than of those you play in late position.

Tip No. 4: Don't overrate suited hands. Having two cards of the same suit definitely makes your hand better, but many beginning players tend to overrate the value of suited cards. In short, a hand like ten-six almost always should be thrown away, whether it is suited or not.

Tip No. 5: High cards are much better than low cards. It's just as easy to make a pair when you have high cards as it is when you have low cards. If you hold

your opponent has

and both of you flop a pair, you have the better hand.
Consequently, you would prefer to have your hand made
up of big cards.

STARTING HANDS

There are five categories of hold'em starting hands that
we will discuss: big pairs, small and medium pairs, two high
cards, suited connectors, and big-little suited. Most other
hands should be thrown away, unless you have the big blind
and the pot has not been raised.

Category No. 1: Big pairs. A pair of tens and higher is
an excellent starting hand. With a high pair, you not only
can make an even bigger hand, but also can completely
miss the board — that is, your hand does not improve —
and still have a reasonable opportunity to win the pot.
Obviously, the chances of winning with two aces are better
than the chances of winning with two tens. In general,
however, all high pairs have immediate value and should be
played aggressively.

Category No. 2: Small and medium pairs. In hold'em, as in seven-card stud, there is a big difference in strength between big pairs and smaller pairs. A hand like

seldom wins the pot without improvement. Moreover, the odds against this hand improving to three of a kind on the flop are almost 8-to-1 (although you still can flop a straight draw).

Since small and medium pairs rarely win without improving, they have little immediate value and therefore can be classified as drawing hands. And to profitably play these hands, you need several opponents in the pot.

Category No. 3: Two high cards. Two unsuited high cards is usually a playable hand but not a great hand. Even though ace-king almost always should be played, a hand like

often should be folded, especially if someone has raised. In addition, this hand must hit the flop to win in a multiway pot.

If your hand is suited, you should be more inclined to play. But remember the warning given earlier: Don't overrate the value of two suited cards.

Category No. 4: Suited connectors. Hands like

are only fair at best. And if your hand contains a gap, you cannot play it as often since your straight possibilities have decreased. This type of hand usually should be thrown away in early position, and you should not call a raise even from a late position unless many players are already in the pot.

Category No. 5: Big-little suited. An ace or a king with a small card of the same suit is similar in value to the suited connectors and should be played as such. In addition, it's wise to remember that ace-little suited is better than king-little suited.

STARTING HAND QUIZ

1. What hands are you primarily interested in playing?
   Big pairs and high cards, especially suited high cards.

2. How do you play these hands?
   Aggressively. Almost always raise, and with the better hands, usually reraise.

3. Suppose two players are already in the pot. The first player has raised, the second has called, and you hold two kings. What should you do?
   Raise again. You have a strong hand and would prefer to shut out the remaining players.

4. In what situation do small pairs play best?
   In a many-handed pot.

5. When you play a small pair, what are you hoping to do?
   To make three of a kind on the flop.

6. When do suited connectors play best?
   When many opponents are in the pot.

7. You are in one of the blind positions, someone has raised, and there are several callers. What kind of hands should you play?
   All of the good hands, plus all pairs and many of the hands that can make straights and flushes.

8. Which hand is better, ace-jack offsuit or eight-seven suited?
   Normally, ace-jack offsuit is the better hand. But when a lot of players are in the pot, you would prefer to hold the eight-seven suited. In this situation, don't overplay a hand like ace-jack.

9. If there is no raise, what hands do you call with out of the little blind?
   Even though you can get in for only a partial bet, you still need to be somewhat selective. Routinely playing hands like

   eventually will prove costly. In other words, you still should discard your worst hands.

10. If someone has raised, how does this affect the hands you should play?
   Generally, you need to be much more selective. Small pairs and medium suited connectors do not play well against a large pair, and when someone raises, he is

quite likely to be holding a large pair. In addition, a raise makes it doubtful that a lot of players will enter the pot. This means you will not get the implied odds — the amount of money you anticipate winning versus the amount you expect it to cost you — that many hands require to be profitable.

11. When should you play a hand like king-four suited?
When you are in a late position, several players are already in, and the pot has not been raised.

12. When you have a close decision regarding whether to play a hand, what should you consider?
In hold'em, as in seven-card stud and all other forms of poker, you must take into account how well those opponents already in the pot play. The better they play, the less inclined you should be to go up against them.

PLAY AFTER THE FLOP

As we mentioned earlier, your starting hand decision in Texas hold'em, though very important, is not the dominating factor that it is in seven-card stud. To be a winner at hold'em, you must play well not only before the flop, but also on the flop and beyond. If your play on the later streets is poor, the best you can hope for is to break even. Following are a few tips that will help you make the correct decisions for play after the flop, which in turn will largely determine your overall success in this complex game.

Tip No. 1: Bet most of your draws. Suppose you have two suited cards and two more of your suit flop, giving you a flush draw. You usually should bet this hand. (If you don't bet, you almost always should call.) Even though your flush draw currently has no value, betting gives you two ways to win the pot. First, everyone might fold immediately, and second, the flush card might come and you will win anyway.

Tip No. 2: If you don't improve on the flop, be willing to abandon your hand. Suppose you are dealt

Even though this is a good starting hand, there is no guarantee that it will be worth very much once the flop comes. If that is the case, you should abandon it immediately. Failure to do so can prove quite costly.

Tip No. 3: It is sometimes necessary to throw away a big pair. When you hold a big pair, you often don't need to improve your hand to win. But sometimes the flop will be so detrimental that you should fold. For example, suppose you hold

in a seven-handed pot, the flop comes

and there is a bet, a raise, and three callers. Under these circumstances, you should throw your hand away, as there are too many ways that you are beat.

Tip No. 4: In multiway pots, be aware that you might be drawing dead. Suppose the flop is

and you hold

Even though you are trying to make a straight — which is often a very strong hand — you may already be beat by a player who has either jack-seven or queen-jack for a higher straight. In addition, if a jack hits the board, anyone holding a queen will beat you. Clearly, you should throw your hand away in this spot if you are against several opponents.

Tip No. 5: Discard small pairs when they miss the flop. Remember, when you play a small pair, you generally must improve to three of a kind. If you don't improve, your hand has little value and usually should be mucked. As emphasized earlier, the odds against making trips on the flop are almost 8-to-1.

Tip No. 6: If you flop a flush draw and a pair also flops, you usually should continue to play. When a pair flops, there is an increased chance that you will run into a full house if you make your flush. Even so, the odds against making your flush with two cards to come are only 2-to-1, and a typical pot offers much more than this.

A SAMPLE HAND

Because of the community cards, Texas hold'em can produce some unusual hands, and many combinations can be out. So if you fail to pay attention to the board and the prior action, you might mistakenly think you have the winner, when in fact, several other players easily can be holding better hands.

Here's an example. Suppose the board is

and you hold

Although you have top pair, which is often a winning hand, if you are against someone who holds he will beat you with two pair. And if another player has

his trips will beat the two pair. In addition, two possible straights can be out. So if another opponent holds

and still another has

then both of these hands will beat the three tens, but the ace-high straight is, of course, the better of the two. And finally, if someone plays he will win the pot with a spade flush.

Incidentally, you normally shouldn't play a hand like 8♠3♠. But some people do, and this is one of the variables that makes the games good. You also must remember that situations like the one just described do occur, and sometimes you have to throw away a good hand.

SPREAD LIMIT STRATEGY CHANGES

The two primary strategy changes provided for spread-limit seven-card stud games are also appropriate for Texas hold'em games played with spread limits. That is, first of all, you often can see the flop cheaply. This means that you should play a few more hands for the minimum amount, which in a typical $1-$4-$8 hold'em game is either $1 or $2. Again, you should consider your position before entering the pot, and if an opponent raises after you have called the blind, you usually should throw away a weak hand.

And second, if you have a good starting hand, you want some competition. So here again, you usually shouldn't raise the maximum before the flop if no one has yet voluntarily entered the pot. Winning only the blind(s) when you hold pocket kings is not your objective.

SELECTED ODDS

As already pointed out, it is not essential to know the exact odds but only to have a general idea of what your chances are in a particular situation. So like the odds furnished for seven-card stud, those that follow for Texas hold'em are provided primarily for their interest alone.

The First Two Cards

Starting Hand	Odds
A Pair of Aces	220-to-1
Any Pair	16-to-1
Two Suited Cards 10 or Higher	32-to-1
Two Unsuited Cards 10 or Higher	10-to-1

Other Odds of Interest

- If you start with two suited cards, the odds against flopping a flush are 118-to-1, while the odds against flopping two flush cards are 8.1-to-1.

- If you flop a four flush, the odds against completing your flush are 1.9-to-1.

- If you start with a pair, the odds against flopping three of a kind are 7.5-to-1.

- If you start with cards of two different ranks, the odds against flopping one pair are 2.7-to-1, the odds against flopping two pair are 48-to-1, and the odds against flopping three of a kind are 73-to-1.

Other Games

INTRODUCTION

So far, we have discussed the two most common forms of poker — namely, seven-card stud and Texas hold'em. But many additional types of poker are played in the cardrooms of Nevada and California, as well as in other places where poker is legal.

In this section, we will examine five of these additional games: Omaha hold'em, Omaha eight-or-better, seven-card stud eight-or-better, razz, and lowball draw. Most, though not all, of these games are actually variations of the two games already covered, so much of the material previously presented will apply. Nevertheless, each form of poker is unique, and strategy requirements vary from game to game.

OMAHA HOLD'EM

The rules for Omaha hold'em are identical to those for standard Texas hold'em, with two exceptions. First, you are dealt four cards instead of two cards, and second, you must use two cards from your hand and three cards from the board to form a five-card poker hand.

Until you become familiar with Omaha, the second rule variation can be troublesome, so you must be careful when evaluating your hand. For example, if four hearts appear on the board but you have only one heart in your hand, you do not have a flush.

Because Omaha is a game that yields many different combinations of cards, it's common for someone to be holding the nuts. There is also more short-term luck in Omaha than in standard Texas hold'em. Nevertheless, the best players still get the chips in the long run.

Tip No. 1: In general, you should play only those hands in which all four cards are coordinated. Since Omaha produces numerous card combinations, the best hands are those where all four cards are working together. This harmonious relationship gives you more opportunities to flop a strong hand, plus sometimes allows you to outdraw an opponent when he happens to flop the same hand that you flop.

Hands you should play include the following:
- Two pair, as long as both pair are eights or higher
- Four cards to a straight with no more than two gaps, such as

- Ace-king double suited to two small cards, like

Tip No. 2: In late position, you can play some weaker hands in an unraised pot. Being one of the last players to act gives you a significant advantage, so if the pot has not been raised, you can play some weaker hands. In fact, in many of these situations, you would require that only three of your cards be well-coordinated.

Tip No. 3: To continue playing on the flop, you need either the nuts or a draw at the nuts. Anyone who plays Omaha for even a short period of time quickly learns that the best possible hand is often out. Consequently, when the flop comes, you want the nuts or a draw at the nuts. Drawing to a hand that easily can be beat — such as a queen-high flush — places you in jeopardy and can prove very expensive.

Tip No. 4: If you flop the best hand but have nothing else to go with it, you should exercise caution. In most Omaha games, many players participate in each pot. This means that when you flop the best possible hand, there is a good chance that an opponent also has made the nuts. So if your hand has no other potential, the best you can hope for in this case is to split the pot. More likely, however, the worst will happen; someone will make a better hand and win the pot.

Here's an example. Suppose the flop is

and you hold queen-jack. At the moment, you have the best possible hand. But any heart can give someone a flush, and if the board pairs, someone can make a full house or even four of a kind. In addition, should a jack or a queen fall, an opponent can make a straight higher than your straight. You should therefore proceed with caution if you flop the nuts but your hand has no other possibilities.

Tip No. 5: If you flop the nuts and have redraws, be willing to gamble. Suppose with the flop just given that you hold a pair of nines to go along with the queen-jack. Now your hand is significantly better, for if the board pairs, you still could win with a full house. You therefore should be more inclined to gamble it up.

Tip No. 6: Bottom set in a multiway pot can be very expensive. Although three of a kind is frequently a good hand, if your trips represent the smallest card on the flop, you often are looking at a hand that can be quite costly — especially if many players have taken the flop. Not only is there a good chance that a bigger set is out, but also any overcard that comes on a later street may beat you.

OMAHA EIGHT-OR-BETTER

Omaha eight-or-better is a split-pot game. The best high hand wins half the pot, and the best low hand wins the other half, as long as the low hand consists of five cards of different ranks, with no card being higher than an eight. Straights and flushes are ignored for low, and the ace can be used as the lowest card.

It is also possible to win both the high and the low — known as scooping the pot — and this is the primary objective when playing Omaha eight-or-better. As in regular Omaha, you must use two cards from your hand and three cards from the board. However, your high hand can be a different five-card combination from that used to make your low hand.

Tip No. 1: Play hands containing ace-deuce, ace-trey, or four big cards. Hands that include ace-deuce or ace-trey are usually playable, although an ace-trey with nothing else frequently should be thrown away from an early position. Four big cards are also good starting hands, and they are exceptionally good when a pair is involved.

Tip No. 2: In late position, you can play some weaker hands in an unraised pot. Acting last provides you with an opportunity to win more money when you get a lucky flop. This means that you should play some weaker hands from a late position, as long as you can get in cheaply and your hand has some value. For example, you normally should throw away

But in a very late position in an unraised pot, hands like this can be played.

Tip No. 3: Don't play medium-sized cards. The problem with playing medium-sized cards is that you can't make the nuts, barring an occasional exception. In addition, when you flop what looks like a good hand, you usually are putting out some low cards. As a result, you're likely at best to split the pot.

Tip No. 4: To continue playing on the flop, you need either the nuts or a draw at the nuts. As in standard Omaha, the best possible hand is often out in Omaha eight-or-better — especially for low. This means that drawing to a trey-deuce low when there is not an ace on board can be expensive. So unless you flop the nuts or a draw to the nuts, you should muck your hand.

Tip No. 5: High hands lose value against low hands. Once three low cards appear on board, your high hand has lost most of its value. Not only will someone holding a low win half the pot, but you can lose the high to a straight as well. For example, suppose you have a pair of eights in your hand and an eight flops, along with two other small cards. Although you now have trips, it's probable that an opponent either already has made a straight or has a straight draw. In this situation, you do not have a strong hand.

Tip No. 6: Turn your cards face up when the hand is over. Many hands are difficult to read in Omaha eight-or-better, especially if you are new to the game. By allowing the dealer to read your hand, you won't mistakenly discard the winner.

SEVEN-CARD STUD EIGHT-OR-BETTER

Seven-card stud eight-or-better is another split-pot game. As noted earlier, the best high hand wins half the pot, and the best low hand wins the other half, as long as the low hand qualifies by containing five cards of different ranks, with no card being higher than an eight. Again, straights and flushes are ignored for low, and the ace can be used as the lowest card. It also is possible in this game to win both the high and the low.

The rules for seven-card stud eight-or-better are identical to those for standard seven-card stud, with one exception: If someone makes an open pair on fourth street, there usually is no option to make a double-sized bet. Only the small bet can be made.

Tip No. 1: Play hands that have the potential to scoop the pot. The best starting hands are rolled-up trips, two aces with a low card, three small cards to a straight or flush, and three small cards that include an ace. All of these hands have a good chance to win the pot both ways, which means that they usually should be played aggressively.

Tip No. 2: The best high hand on third street is also a good starting hand. A hand like a pair of kings also has a good chance to scoop, since the low must make at least an eight to be eligible for half the pot. However, if several players with low cards showing have already entered the pot, many high hands lose much of their value. Playing for half the pot against an opponent with a made low, who also may have a draw at a high hand that will beat you, can be a costly error.

Tip No. 3: The second best high hand on third street should be discarded. Even though the best high hand is usually a good starting hand, the second best high hand should be thrown away. You don't want to play a pair of queens when you are against a likely pair of kings.

Tip No. 4: When an ace raises, you should play very few hands. Suppose you have a big pair. If an ace raises, you can't take the chance that you might be against a pair of aces. And even if your opponent has only three low cards, he still can catch an ace to beat you. To play in this situation, you need three very good low cards.

Tip No. 5: One-way low hands, especially heads up, have little value. Suppose you are against a high hand, and you are going for low with no chance to make a high. You will win either half the pot or nothing. If your opponent is likely to make you put a lot of bets into the pot on the remaining streets, you should throw away most one-way low hands, unless the pot is already quite large.

Tip No. 6: If it is early in the hand and someone is favored over you, no matter what the direction, usually fold. When you are not a favorite to win at least one way, and the pot is still small, throw your hand away. There is one important exception: If your hand has even a small chance to win both ways, you should continue to play. For example, if you have four cards to a medium straight, such as

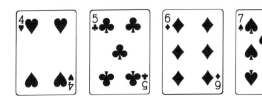

and it appears that you are against a high pair and a better low draw, you should keep playing.

RAZZ

Razz is seven-card stud played for low. The best possible hand, known as a wheel or a bicycle, is ace-deuce-trey-four-five. Straights and flushes do not count. The rules for razz are the same as those for seven-card stud, with two exceptions. First, the player with the highest card on third street starts the action, and second, the player with the lowest board on each subsequent round is first to act.

Tip No. 1: Most hands with three small cards are playable. Determining a playable hand in razz is simple. You need three cards of different ranks, with no card being higher than an eight. Keep in mind that the ace counts as the lowest card. The only exception to playing three small cards is when you have an eight as your upcard and several small cards remain to act behind you. In this case, you might want to fold.

Tip No. 2: Three cards to a wheel is a very strong starting hand and should be played as such. Any time you have three different ranks of cards lower than a six, you have a very strong starting hand. Always raise, and if someone already has raised, you should reraise.

Tip No. 3: If you catch a bad card on fourth street and your opponent catches a good card, throw away your hand. If you catch a face card on fourth street and your opponent catches a small card, you should discard your hand, even though the small card might have paired your opponent. The only exceptions to this rule are if you started with an unusually strong hand or if a lot of money is already in the pot.

Tip No. 4: A one-card draw to a wheel or a six is a favorite over a made nine-eight on fifth street. If you have four cards to a wheel or a six, and your opponent has

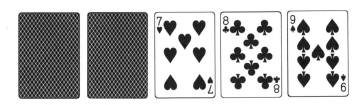

you are a small favorite. So if he checks to you, you should bet, and if he bets, you should raise.

Tip No. 5: If you go to sixth street, you almost always should go to the river. In razz, as in standard seven-card stud, if you take a card on sixth street, you generally should go to the river. The pot usually has become large enough by now that you need only a small chance to win for your call to be correct. The only exception to calling is if you think your opponent has caught perfect and you have no chance to win.

Tip No. 6: Bluff on the end if you have three or four low cards showing and your opponent needed to catch a good card to make his hand. Even if your hand actually has little value, if you have three or four low cards showing, it appears as though you have a made hand. By the same token, if your opponent has two low cards and two high cards on board, he obviously was drawing to a decent low. In this situation, you should bluff virtually every time. Unless your opponent has caught a good card, he will have difficulty justifying a call with something like a queen for low.

LOWBALL DRAW

So far we have discussed many different variations of open poker. But one variation of closed poker is still widely played in some of the cardrooms in California, where only closed poker was legal until 1987. This game is lowball draw, also known as California lowball or ace-to-five draw.

The structure of lowball draw varies widely, depending on where the game is played and the limit that is played. But most games have one or more blinds, and some games — especially those at the lower limits — require each player to make a small ante.

The deck used for lowball draw consists of the standard 52 cards, plus a joker, which counts as the lowest card not already in your hand. Each player is dealt five cards. There is then a round of betting, after which those players who remain can either stand pat — that is, not draw any cards — or draw from one to five cards. A final round of betting then takes place. If two or more players remain after the final round of betting, the hands are shown down, and the lowest hand wins — with ace-deuce-trey-four-five being the best possible hand. As in razz, straights and flushes do not count.

Also, one additional rule is unique to lowball draw: the "must bet sevens" rule. This rule states that if you have made a seven or better after the draw, you must bet it or you forfeit any additional action. For example, if you make a seven and then check and call, you cannot win the after-the-draw bet, even if your hand is good.

Tip No. 1: Don't fall in love with the joker. The best card to have in lowball draw is obviously the joker, and it definitely makes your hand stronger. But holding the joker doesn't mean that your hand is automatically playable. Many other factors must be considered before entering the pot.

Tip No. 2: In an early position, you need at least a seven-five to draw to if you don't hold the joker. If you are in an early position, many players still remain to act behind you, plus you must act before they do after the draw. Consequently, to play in this spot, you need a fairly good hand. This restricts you to a one-card draw to at least a seven-five.

Tip No. 3: If you have the joker, you can draw to any seven up front. Holding the joker makes a significant difference. You now can catch more cards that will make your hand, and you hold fewer cards that can pair. In addition, the fact that you hold the joker means that no one else can have it.

Tip No. 4: Don't play a pat nine up front. If you hold 9-8-6-5-4 in an early position, throw it away. If you are dealt 9-5-4-3-2 up front, usually play it as a one-card draw to a wheel. The only exception is when you are against the blind, who acts before you do, and he draws two cards. In this case, you can stand pat.

Tip No. 5: You can draw to weak hands in the late positions, providing that you are the first player to enter the pot. There are two reasons for this. First, you are not as likely to run into a good hand. Second, if you do get action, it probably will be from one of the blinds, and you will have position over him after the draw. You can even play a two-card draw if you are first in from a very late position.

Tip No. 6: When first in from any position, almost always raise. There are two reasons for raising. First, you may pick up the blinds if no one else plays. Second, in lowball, unless you start with a very strong hand, your edge over an opponent — even if he draws several cards — is not that great. Thus you don't want to give anyone in the blind a free shot at you.

Tip No. 7: If someone else has already entered the pot, your minimum playing hand should be the minimum hand you would play if you were first in from that position. For example, if someone raises up front, you can call with

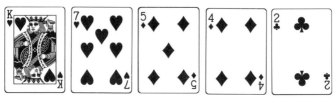

but you should throw away

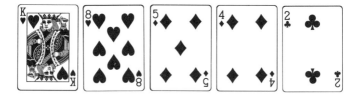

Tip No. 8: Usually reraise with a draw to a six or better or with any pat hand that you are going to play. Any draw to a six or better is a strong hand, and you should play it as such. However, the reason you reraise with some of your weaker pat hands is to drive out the competition, as these hands play best against only one opponent.

Tip No. 9: After the draw, be willing to bet your bigger pairs. When you make a hand like a pair of eights, the only way you can win is to bluff. So usually bet them, especially if you are first to act.

Tip No. 10: When you are first to act in a heads-up pot after the draw, usually bet if your hand is a nine or better. Exceptions to this are if your opponent did not draw any cards or if the action before the draw indicated that he was drawing to a very strong hand. You will lose a lot of these bets, but against typical players, they will show a profit in the long run.

Tip No. 11: When you are last to act in a heads-up pot after the draw and it is checked to you, usually bet if your hand is a ten-eight or better. Again, an exception is if your opponent is playing a pat hand. Otherwise, these bets should show a profit over the long term.

Conclusion

As you have seen, poker in its many forms is both a simple and a very complex game. It's simple in that almost everyone can learn the basics of any poker game in just a few minutes. After a short period of time, some people will even believe that they play very well. But in fact, poker is extraordinarily complex. It takes a long time to become an expert, no matter what game you choose to play, as many of the strategy decisions required are quite sophisticated.

But whether you're a novice or an expert, poker is fun to play. And because the substantial luck element in the game can be balanced by a high level of skill, poker is exciting, challenging, and rewarding.

Remember, this booklet will not make you a champion. We hope, however, that it will get you started in the right direction and enable you to hold your own in the small limit games. If this is the case — and if you do your homework — you just might become a future poker star.

Glossary

All in: When all of a player's money (or chips) on the table is put into the pot.

Ante: A token bet required before the start of a hand.

Bet: To voluntarily put money or chips into the pot.

Blind: A forced bet that one or more players must make before any cards are dealt to start the action on the first round of betting.

Bluff: To bet or raise with a hand that is unlikely to be the best hand.

Board: In Texas hold'em and similar games, the five cards that are turned face up in the center of the table; in seven-card stud and variations thereof, the four cards that are dealt face up to each player.

Bring-in: The forced bet made on the first betting round by the player dealt the lowest card showing in seven-card stud and the highest card showing in razz.

Button: In Texas hold'em and similar games, a small disk that signifies the player in last position when a house dealer is used.

Call: To put into the pot an amount of money equal to an opponent's bet or raise.

Check: To abstain from betting, but to remain in contention for the pot.

Closed poker: Games in which all of the cards are dealt face down.

Community cards: In hold'em and similar games, the cards dealt face up in the center of the table that are shared by all active players.

Door card: In seven-card stud, the first exposed card in a player's hand.

Drawing dead: Drawing to a hand that cannot possibly win.

Fifth street: In Texas hold'em and similar games, the final round of betting and the fifth community card on board; in seven-card stud and its variations, the fifth card dealt to each player and the third betting round (on the third upcard).

Flop: In hold'em, the first three community cards, which are turned face up simultaneously and start the second round of betting.

Flush: Five cards of the same suit.

Fourth street: In hold'em, the fourth card on board and the third round of betting; in seven-card stud, the fourth card dealt to each player and the second round of betting (on the second upcard).

Implied odds: The amount of money you expect to win if you make your hand versus the amount of money it will cost you to continue playing.

Kicker: A side card.

Live card: In stud games, a card that has not yet been seen and is therefore presumed likely to be still in play.

Loose game: A game with a lot of players in most pots.

Muck: To discard a hand.

Nuts: The best possible hand at any given point.

Open poker: Games where some of the cards are dealt face up.

Overcard: In seven-card stud, a card higher than the rank of your opponent's probable pair; in hold'em, a card higher than any card on the flop.

Pot: The money or chips placed in the center of the table.

Pot odds: The amount of money in the pot versus the amount of money it will cost you to continue in the hand.

Raise: To bet an additional amount after someone else has bet.

Redraw: A draw to an even better hand when you currently are holding the nuts.

River: In hold'em, the last round of betting on the fifth-street card; in stud, the last round of betting on the seventh-street card.

Rolled up: In seven-card stud, three of a kind on third street.

Rush: Several winning hands in a short period of time.

Scare card: An upcard that looks as though it might have made a strong hand.

Set: Three of a kind.

Seventh street: The final betting round on the last card in seven-card stud.

Sixth street: In seven-card stud, the fourth round of betting on the sixth card.

Straight: Five cards of mixed suits in sequence.

Suited: Cards of the same suit; used to describe two-card combinations in hold'em or the first three cards in seven-card stud.

Third street: In seven-card stud, the first round of betting on the first three cards.

Three flush: In seven-card stud, a starting hand consisting of three suited cards.

Tight game: A game with a small number of players in most pots.

Top pair: In hold'em, pairing the highest card on board.

Trips: Three of a kind.

Turn: In hold'em, the fourth-street card.

Recommended Reading

The purpose of this booklet is to provide you with the basic strategy for playing a wide variety of poker games. It is not designed to make you an expert player. Becoming a champion requires an enormous amount of study, coupled with a great deal of experience at the poker table. This process can be accelerated, however, by absorbing the information available in a number of excellent poker books. In fact, should you become a serious student of the game, you will find the few books that follow essential to your success.

- *Hold'em Poker* by David Sklansky
- *Hold'em Poker For Advanced Players* by David Sklansky and Mason Malmuth
- *Seven-Card Stud For Advanced Players* by David Sklansky, Mason Malmuth, and Ray Zee
- *High-Low-Split Poker, Seven-Card Stud and Omaha Eight-or-Better For Advanced Players* by Ray Zee
- *The Theory of Poker* by David Sklansky
- *Super System* by Doyle Brunson
- *Omaha Hold'em Poker — "The Action Game"* by Bob Ciaffone
- *Sklansky on Poker* by David Sklansky
- *Poker Essays* by Mason Malmuth
- *Mike Caro's Book of Tells* by Mike Caro
- *Mike Caro's Fundamental Secrets of Poker* by Mike Caro

All of these books are available from dealers that specialize in gaming literature, including:

Gambler's Book Club
630 South 11th Street
Las Vegas, NV 89101
(702) 382-7555 ● (800) 634-6243

Gambler's General Store
800 South Main Street
Las Vegas, NV 89101
(702) 382-9903

Gambler's Bookstore
99 N. Virginia Street
Reno, NV 89501
(702) 786-6209 ● (800) 748-5797

Gambler's Mail Order Store
P.O. Box C-14986
Las Vegas, NV 89114
(702) 734-6089

Atlantic City News and Books
101 South Illinois Ave.
Atlantic City, NJ 08401
(609) 344-9444

Gambler's World
1938 E. University Drive
Tempe, AZ 85281
(602) 968-2590

Rocky Mountain Gaming Books & Supplies, Inc.
1931 Sheridan (Unit: V)
Edgewater, CO 80214
(303) 232-1077

Gambling Books Plus
3661 S. Maryland Parkway
Las Vegas, NV 89109
(702) 796-0130 ● (800) 676-0130

Casino Wheels & Deals
1520 E. Algonquin Rd.
Arlington Heights, IL 60005
(708) 228-9021

ABOUT THE AUTHORS

Mason Malmuth *is a professional mathematician who became interested in gambling in the late 1970s and has become recognized as one of the leading authorities in this field. Today, Mason doesn't do very much, but he occasionally can be found at the poker tables in either Las Vegas or Southern California.*

__Lynne Loomis__ has been a professional freelance writer and editor for 20 years and has written countless articles on gambling and other industry-related topics. She also occasionally can be found in casinos and cardrooms around the country. But since Mason is lazy and doesn't do very much, Lynne is the working half of their collaborations.

Notes